Sarah Lauren Wahl

C000000208

JUDITH
WRIGHT

Phantom Dwelling

VIRAGO

Other poetry volumes by Judith Wright

The Moving Image – Woman to Man
The Gateway – The Two Fires – Birds
Five Senses – Selected Poems – The Other Half
Collected Poems – Alive – Fourth Quarter

Acknowledgements

Some of the poems in this collection have been
published in *Landfall, Outposts, Poetry Australia,
Simply Living, The Age, Luna, Gumleaves, Cross-
Canada Writers' Quarterly*, and *Journal of
Literature and Aesthetics* (South India).

Published by VIRAGO PRESS Limited 1986
41 William IV Street, London WC2N 4DB

First published in Australia
by Angus & Robertson Publishers in 1985

Copyright © Judith Wright 1985

All rights reserved

British Library Cataloguing in Publication Data
Wright, Judith
  Phantom dwelling.
  I. Title
  821   PR9619.3.W/

  ISBN 0-86068-747-3

Printed in Great Britain by
Anchor Brendon, Tiptree, Essex

Contents

Four Poems from New Zealand

i *From the Wellington Museum*

Vine-spiralling Maori genealogies,
carved paths through forests
inscribed with life-forms, coded histories
tangled my eyes
never quite able to meet that paua-stare.

Outside the museum
(built, like the city, on a fault-line,
they keep on telling you)
the city climbs and scrabbles,
arguing with contours, trying to keep square.

Having dropped out of the sky
to get here, I knew the double fetch of oceans
belting a narrow land. Ridged peaking crawls
of alps topped neat with sundae-snow.
Surge. Pressure. Cracks of farmland
scattered with wool-worms,
sheepyards, wooden houses.

The city's only joke, winds tweak
hair into watering eyes.
Rain-blows whip up the bay.

A grizzled man, scotch-eyed, grey-overcoated
stares from the terrace. A straggle of Maori boys
come swinging curls and tangles. Packs
cling like children on their backs.
Around his donegal-granite stance
their laughter parts, loops out
like water spiralling around a stone.

This sky flies clouds, gulls, ghosts.
Deep down, the world-plates struggle
in strangling quiet on each other.
Offshore, deliberate breakers hit the coasts.

Gashes of wind on green-scummed water.
Gnawed terraces shelve the scoria hills,
the sea a hidden theme
beyond the dunes. Gorse, bracken, blackberries
scab over wounded ground.

Suddenly here an ancient crack of valley
left to itself, its cloak of darkgreen feathers
trembling with wind, drops down beside the rails.

Over the forest names
the Maoris left, they have imposed
another country's history
(Palmerston North, New Plymouth).
Over the bared and crumbling hills
sheep eat, eat, eat and trot dementedly.

In small towns, tea-rooms
are called White Heather, Dewdrop Inn.
On rainy stations, pinkfaced countrywomen
drag children wrapped in wool.
Sometimes the softeyed longhaired young
run hand in hand carrying hikers' packs.
COME ALIVE, the poster tells them.

Most birds in these square farmlands
are sparrows, skylarks, starlings.
Just once I see, hawking a narrow river,
one flash, kingfisher-blue.

Such kind uncertain ladies in their best
gather to entertain the visitor.
The local talent stands by the piano
fingering music-pages
criss-crossed with sticky-tape.
They sing 'I Love You Truly'
to an audience in neat and nervous rows.
This district
'is essentially one of clean sentiment',
declared the Tourist Bureau publication.

The town, however, was christened
in honour of an Elizabethan playwright
whose sentiments were often questionable.
Much farther south,
another questionable poet, Burns,
broods on another town.

Politely introduced, I lose my terror.
I read them Alec Hope:
age. Passion. Loss, and death.

They lean a little forward. Faces answer,
'We too have not much time
to find the one in whose lost folds of hair
we long to sleep. Here too the early snows
have already fallen.'

The single terrible white peak
rears in the window-frame.
It is for tourists. Just a tourist-mountain.
'But sometimes, we too pause
and look, and look away.'
So white, it casts a shadow on the day.

A narrow shelf below the southern alps,
a slate-grey beach scattered with drifted wood
darkens the sullen jade
of Tasman's breakers. Blackbacked gulls
hunt the green turn of waves.

One girl with Maori eyes
gathers up driftwood for a winter fire.
But for her smile, the beach is bare.
I am a one-day stranger here,

not knowing even the gulls' language.
I hawk their beach too, looking for momentos
(as the souvenir shops wisely spell it.)
A coppery log, a Maori twine of roots —
can't carry that.

Behind me, the sky's paled
by a swoop of mountains, scope of snow
northward and southward. Jags, saw-teeth, blades of light
nobody could inhabit. Not my country.
I go back to my loves, my proper winter.

Here in the chant of sea-edge, grind of shingle,
I choose one stone,
a slate-grey oval scrawled with quartz
like a foam-edge, an edge of mountains
white as my hair.

I take you this for love, for being alone;
for being, itself. Being that's ground by glaciers,
seas and time. Out of the sea's teeth
I chose it for you, for another country,
loving you, loving another country.

POEMS 1978–1980

Backyard

Knifed with green-glowing blades
and scissor-striped with shade
this square of grass and pioneering weed
frequented by blue moth, white butterfly
is forest level with my eye
where travellers toil and hurry. I
focus in closer, trying to live there too,
or switchback up from birdshadow to sky.

Blake's ancient men
blow-bearded spheres of feather-grey
rear on their dying stem,
loosening parachutes of dangling seed
and set them flying spiderwise.
Swung in parabolas they sink and rise,
halting on dock and thistle, burr, plantain;
glider-observers of terrain
where beetles blunder through a sorrel maze.

Autumn swings earth round sun
at the invisible lasso's end,
turning this latitude south and winterward.
This scrap of surface knows what's going on
and has its orders memorised.
Feed, pack and swaddle seed; store in the root
food to see the winter out;
prepare your planned retreat.
Ants hurry harvests underground.
Earth-dwellers scout
and burrow cells exactly larva-sized.

In last alchemic leaves held to the light,
in soundless bursts of seed,
in the tough satin of the spider's case
and the foam-plastic comb the mantis lays,
in branched green-copper-scaly spires of dock
the season's shorthand coils its final code;
This treeless trampled scrap of earth
fibrous with rot and weed
repeats its ancient orders. Use all death
to feed all life. The lockup of the frost
will melt, the codes translate with nothing lost.

Smalltown Dance

Two women find the square-root of a sheet.
That is an ancient dance:
arms wide: together: again: two forward steps: hands meet
your partner's once and twice.
That white expanse
reduces to a neat
compression fitting in the smallest space
a sheet can pack in on a cupboard shelf.

High scented walls there were of flapping white
when I was small, myself.
I walked between them, playing Out of Sight.
Simpler than arms, they wrapped and comforted —
clean corridors of hiding, roofed with blue —
saying, Your sins too are made Monday-new;
and see, ahead
that glimpse of unobstructed waiting green.
Run, run before you're seen.

But women know the scale of possibility,
the limit of opportunity,
the fence,
how little chance
there is of getting out. The sheets that tug
sometimes struggle from the peg,
don't travel far. Might symbolise
something. Knowing where danger lies
you have to keep things orderly.
The household budget will not stretch to more.

And they can demonstrate it in a dance.
First pull those wallowing white dreamers down,
spread arms: then close them. Fold
those beckoning roads to some impossible world,
put them away and close the cupboard door.

Late Meeting

The last, the very last
flower of the autumn
lifts its too-pale
head in the wind from the snows.

The last, the very last
journey from the hive
tempts out the wind-worn bee.

They meet, they mingle,
tossed by the chilly air
in the old ecstasy,

as though
nothing existed past
the moment's joining,

as though
from this late take-and-give
some seed might set.

His dimming faceted eyes
reflect a thin
near-winter sunlight,

the gusts of wind
tremble her petals round him,
a failing shelter.

End of a Monarchy

The sunset's classical crater
erupts. Billows and skeins
of cirrus, cirrostratus,
altocumulus, cumulus
dispose above the plains
their various shapes and altitudes
for the great Irradiator.
Wornout soils from the west
haze upwards in pinkening dust;
clouds take up welcoming attitudes
for the old Big Show to begin.

Reaching edges, cliffs, finality,
it's right to dramatise,
bring in tragedy, comedy, irony,
wear masks for emphasis.
Stamping his life's last stage
the original King, earth's ruler
meets his dark tanist twin
with a crossing of swords, a rage
of purple, scarlet, crimson,
for the death of a day or an age.

We know the end of our play
as a common human ill.
What we get of pomp and ritual
leaks to a final funeral.
No higher court of appeal
will save us, prole and underling,
whatever counsel may say;
but the King is never undone.
A little expedient conjuring
and here he is again. . .

Today, in a different guise,
in a supersonic jet
keeping up with the nuclear set
and the exponential leap.
In a sonic boom of surprise

his multinational vectors
shatter the anxious sleep
of his subjects. Now he is met
at dawn by prime ministers, guards,
and chairmen of directors —
never by priests and bards.

Sun-king, Irradiator,
what does your briefcase hide?
What are the contract's terms?
And supposing the dollars are real
what do we get on the deal?
If we crash, we're broke to the wide.
And you? At the end of the day
when your jet goes west to the Twin
will the last Big Show begin,
the closing night of the play?

Victims

They are ageing now, some dead.
In the third-class suburbs of exile
their foreign accents
continue to condemn them. They should
not have expected more.

They had their time
of blazing across headlines,
welcomes, interviews, placings
in jobs that could not fit,
of being walked round carefully.
One averts the eyes
from horror or miracle equally.

Their faces, common to humankind,
had eyes, lips, noses.
That in itself was grave
seen through such a flame.

The Czech boy, talking,
posturing, desperate to please,
restless as a spastic trying
to confine his twitches
into the normal straitjacket —
what could we do with him?

The neighbours asked him
to children's parties,
being at sixteen a child;
gave him small jobs
having no niche to hold him
whether as icon, inhabitant
or memento mori.
He could not be a person
having once been forced to carry
other children's corpses
to the place of burning.

But when we saw him walk
beside our own children
darkness rose from that pit.
Quickly but carefully
(he must not notice)
we put our bodies
between our children and the Victim.

Absit omen, you gods —
avert the doom,
the future's beckoning flame.

Perhaps he did notice. At last
he went away.

In what backstreet of what city
does he keep silence, unreadable
fading graffito of half-
forgotten obscenity?

Think: such are not to be pitied.
They wear already
a coat of ash seared in.
But our children and their children
have put on, over the years
a delicate cloak of fat.

Brennan

Self-proclaimed companion
of prophets, priests and poets,
walker on earth's last fringes,
haunted lover
of the beckoning darkness,
last Symbolist, poor hero
lost looking for yourself,
your journey was our journey.
This is for you.

History's burning garbage
of myths and searches
sends up its smoke-wreath
from the city dump.
It stings in our eyes too.

Seeking in the flesh of youth
for Eve's spring meadows
of blue and golden flowers,
deep in their centres
you saw the empty question —
the question of the sphinx
half-nature and half-woman.
It mocked, No answer?

Walking the streets of your poem
you told dead Mallarmé
Here's your great book,
finished at the ends of earth.
It's the story of Man. Above you
in the black of Crown Street
the Cross's pointers
directed you in silence
to the pit of darkness
the South Celestial Pole.

In this continent, last-invaded
landfall of the Navigator,
full of survivals; Chimera's
final landing-ground;

you saw the Wanderer's
emptiest, loneliest desert.
On that stage, always pretentious,
you wore the solemn cloak
of old philosopher-kings.
Your ruined hawk-face
shone under your wide hat
reddened with drink.
Your home was the black of Crown Street
the kings being gone.

Lost dog of the end of a story,
black leaf blowing
in a wind of the wrong hemisphere
you died before your death.
Smallest of stars, perhaps,
you cling in the pit of darkness
to the depth of Lilith's hair.

Seasonal Flocking

Last week outside my window
the tree grew red rosellas,
berry-bright fruits, the young ones
brocaded with juvenile green.
I said, the autumn's ending.
They have come out of the mountains
and the snowcloud shadows.

This week on the road to town
in the red-hung hawthorn,
eleven of the Twelve Apostles;
eight black cockatoos, their tails
fanned to show yellow panes,
uncounted magpies and currawongs
greasily fat from the dump and the butcher's throwouts —
that breeding-ground of maggots.

All of them flocked together,
crying aloud, knowing
the end of autumn.
Sharp-edged welcome-swallows
gathered and circled upwards.

Frost soon, and the last warmth passes.
Seed-stems rot on wet grasses.

At the end of autumn
I too — I want you near me,
all you who've gone, who scatter
into far places or are hidden under
summer-forgotten gravestones.

For a Pastoral Family

i *To my brothers*

Over the years, horses have changed to land-rovers.
Grown old, you travel your thousands of acres
deploring change and the wickedness of cities
and the cities' politics; hoping to pass to your sons
a kind of life you inherited in your generation.
Some actions of those you vote for stick in your throats.
There are corruptions one cannot quite endorse;
but if they are in our interests, then of course...

Well, there are luxuries still,
including pastoral silence, miles of slope and hill,
the cautious politeness of bankers. These are owed
to the forerunners, men and women
who took over as if by right a century and a half
in an ancient difficult bush. And after all
the previous owners put up little fight,
did not believe in ownership, and so were scarcely human.

Our people who gnawed at the fringe
of the edible leaf of this country
left you a margin of action, a rural security,
and left to me
what serves as a base for poetry,
a doubtful song that has a dying fall.

ii *To my generation*

A certain consensus of echo, a sanctioning sound,
supported our childhood lives. We stepped
on sure and conceded ground.
A whole society
extended a comforting cover of legality.
The really deplorable deeds
had happened out of our sight, allowing us innocence.
We were not born, or there was silence kept.

If now there are landslides, if our field of reference
is much eroded, our hands show little blood.
We enter a plea: Not Guilty.
For the good of the Old Country,
the land was taken; the Empire had loyal service.
Would any convict us?
Our plea has been endorsed by every appropriate jury.

If my poetic style, your pastoral produce,
are challenged by shifts in the market
or a change of taste, at least we can go down smiling
with enough left in our pockets
to be noted in literary or local histories.

iii *For today*

We were always part of a process. It has expanded.
What swells over us now is a logical spread
from the small horizons we made —
the heave of the great corporations
whose bellies are never full.
What sort of takeover bid
could you knock back now if the miners,
the junk-food firms or their processors want your land?
Or worse, leave you alone to hoe
small beans in a dwindling row?

The fears of our great-grandfathers —
apart from a fall in the English market —
were of spearwood, stone axes. Sleeping
they sprang awake at the crack
of frost on the roof, the yawn and stretching
of a slab wall. We turn on the radio
for news from the U.S.A. and U.S.S.R.
against which no comfort or hope
might come from the cattle prizes at the Show.

Yet a marginal sort of grace
as I remember it, softened our arrogant clan.
We were fairly kind to horses
and to people not too different from ourselves.
Kipling and A. A. Milne were our favourite authors
but Shelley, Tennyson, Shakespeare stood on our shelves —
suitable reading for women,
to whom, after all, the amenities had to be left.

An undiscursive lot (discourse is for the city)
one of us helped to found a university.
We respected wit in others,
though we kept our own for weddings,
unsure of the bona fides of the witty.

In England, we called on relatives,
assuming welcome for the sake of a shared bloodline,
but kept our independence.
We would entertain them equally, if they came
and with equal hospitality —
blood being thicker than thousands of miles of waters —
for the sake of Great-aunt Charlotte and old letters.

At church, the truncate, inarticulate
Anglican half-confession
'there is no health in us'
made us gag a little. We knew we had no betters
though too many were worse.
We passed on the collection-plate
adding a reasonable donation.

That God approved us was obvious.
Most of our ventures were prosperous.
As for the *Dies Irae*
we would deal with that when we came to it.

v *Change*

At best, the men of our clan
have been, or might have been,
like Yeats' fisherman.
A small stream, narrow but clean,

running apart from the world.
Those hills might keep them so,
granite, gentle and cold.
But hills erode, streams go

through settlement and town
darkened by chemical silt.
Dams hold and slow them down,
trade thickens them like guilt.

All men grow evil with trade
as all roads lead to the city.
Willie Yeats would have said,
perhaps, the more the pity.

But how can we be sure?
Wasn't his chosen man
as ignorant as pure?
Keep out? Stay clean? Who can?

Blue early mist in the valley. Apricots
bowing the orchard trees, flushed red with summer,
loading bronze-plaqued branches;
our teeth in those sweet buttock-curves. Remember
the horses swinging to the yards, the smell
of cattle, sweat and saddle-leather?
Blue ranges underlined the sky. In any weather
it was well, being young and simple,
letting the horses canter home together.

All those sights, smells and sounds we shared
trailing behind grey sheep, red cattle,
from Two-rail or Ponds Creek
through tawny pastures breathing pennyroyal.
In winter, sleety winds bit hands and locked
fingers round reins. In spring, the wattle.

With so much past in common,
on the whole we forgive each other
for the ways in which we differ —
two old men, one older woman.
When one of us falls ill,
the others may think less
of today's person, the lined and guarding face,

than of a barefoot child running careless through
long grass where snakes lie, or forgetting
to watch in the paddocks for the black Jersey bull.
Divisions and gulfs deepen
daily, the world over
more dangerously than now between us three.
Which is why, while there is time (though not our form at all)
I put the memories into poetry.

Words, Roses, Stars

(for John Béchervaise, answering a Christmas poem)

A rose, my friend, a rose —
and what's a rose?
A swirl of atoms bodied in a word.
And words are human; language comes and goes
with us, and lives among us. Not absurd
to think the human spans the Milky Way.

Baiame bends beside his crystal stream
shaded beneath his darker cypress-tree
and gives the gift of life, the endless dream,
to Koori people, and to you and me.
Astronomers and physicists compute
a mathematic glory in the sky.
But all those calculations, let's admit,
are filtered through a human brain and eye.

If I could give a rose to you, and you,
it would be language; sight and touch and scent
join in that symbol. Yet the word is true,
plucked by a path where human vision went.

Hunting Snake

Sun-warmed in this late season's grace
under the autumn's gentlest sky
we walked, and froze half-through a pace.
The great black snake went reeling by.

Head-down, tongue flickering on the trail
he quested through the parting grass;
sun glazed his curves of diamond scale,
and we lost breath to watch him pass.

What track he followed, what small food
fled living from his fierce intent,
we scarcely thought; still as we stood
our eyes went with him as he went.

Cold, dark and splendid he was gone
into the grass that hid his prey.
We took a deeper breath of day,
looked at each other, and went on.

Rainforest

The forest drips and glows with green.
The tree-frog croaks his far-off song.
His voice is stillness, moss and rain
drunk from the forest ages long.

We cannot understand that call
unless we move into his dream,
where all is one and one is all
and frog and python are the same.

We with our quick dividing eyes
measure, distinguish and are gone.
The forest burns, the tree-frog dies,
yet one is all and all are one.

NOTES AT EDGE

Brevity

Old Rhythm, old Metre
these days I don't draw
very deep breaths. There isn't
much left to say.

Rhyme, my old cymbal,
I don't clash you as often,
or trust your old promises
of music and unison.

I used to love Keats, Blake.
Now I try haiku
for its honed brevities,
its inclusive silences.

Issa. Shiki. Buson. Bashō.
Few words and with no rhetoric.
Enclosed by silence
as is the thrush's call.

Mountain

Eastward, Mount Budawang
deliberately releases
stars, moon and sun
upward by night or day, one following one;

or rolls out nightly
and daily back again
a scroll and screen of cloud.

By dawn or twilight
it cuts a fine dark figure on the sky —
a lengthened strip of black calligraphy.

Sun-orchid

Sun-orchid, Thelymitra,
what a blue of blues you've chosen
to remind this sullen season
that still the sky is there.

Its tender cherishing colour
is like the hills in summer
when a eucalyptine vapour
dreams up in windless air.

Another poet, staring,
saw the sun in your centre, burning
core of fire, and, dazzled,
closed eyes upon that secret.

Wrapped in your Mary-blue,
veined with a flush like roses,
you stand in contemplation
of a spring as cold as winter,

but, blessed from your creation,
the calm of your robe encloses
a gold like revelation.

Rock

I dug from this shallow soil
a rock-lump square as a book,
split into leaves of clay.

A long curved wash of ripple
left there its fingerprint
one long-before-time lost day.

I turn a dead sea's leaves
stand on a shore of waves
and touch that day, and look.

Fox

That rufous canterer
through my eye's corner
crossing an empty space of frost-red grass
goes running like a flame.

Against storm-black Budawang
a bushfire bristle of brush.
Under the candlebark trees
a rustle in dry litter.

Fox, fox!
Behind him follows the crackle of his name.

Epacris

Grey-green, as high as a hand
beside that lichened stone,
it has clenched pale buds
no bigger than river-sand
while spring and summer passed.

Now as the summer ends,
slowly, day by day,
it opens those ant-sized bells;
their honey harvest, the last
for small black hastening ants
whose nest waits under the stone.

Violet Stick-insects

A landscape of leaves, oblique,
curved to the tension of light;
and among them he and she,
one a leaning twig
one a gnawed thin-bellied leaf.

Eating, they hang
still, or rock with the wind,
one with the branch that moves.

Any shadow might be a beak,
but as twig or leaf they are safe.
Yet he planes on a downward swing
unfolding a brilliant wing —
a fearless violet flash
to centre that grey and green.

River Bend

What killed that kangaroo-doe, slender skeleton
tumbled above the water with her long shanks
cleaned white as moonlight?
Pad-tracks in sand where something drank fresh blood.

Last night a dog howled somewhere,
a hungry ghost in need of sacrifice.

Down by that bend, they say, the last old woman,
thin, black and muttering grief,
foraged for mussels, all her people gone.

The swollen winter river
curves over stone, a wild perpetual voice.

Lichen, Moss, Fungus

Autumn and early winter
wet this clay soil with rains.
Slow primitive plantforms
push up their curious flowers.

Lichens, mosses and fungi —
these flourish on this rock ridge,
a delicate crushable tundra:
bracket, star, cup, parasol,
gilled, pored, spored, membraned,
white, chestnut, violet, red.

I stoke the fire with wood
laced with mycelia, tread
a crust of moss and lichen.
Over the wet decay
of log and fallen branch
there spreads an embroidery, ancient
source of the forests.

Caddis-fly

Small twilight helicopter,
four petals, four skins of crystal
veined taut with chitinous fibre
carry you into my wineglass.
Why such a dying fall?

I sat under leaves, toasting
a simple moon, a river,
the respite of an evening
warm as the hand of a lover.
Did you have to cry Alas?

I lift you out on a finger
dripping red with wine
to dry beside the campfire,
but you won't fly again.

All of a sudden
you gather four wings together,
still drooping, sodden,
and dive to the fire's centre.

Why should I mourn, little buddha,
small drunkard of the flame?
I finish my wine and dream
on your fire-sermon.

Glass Corridor

Down the glass passageway
three of us walk. Left. Right.
and who's in the middle?

That's the lying inventor,
the self-contemplator,
with moonrise on one hand
sunset on the other.

We three walk through
a forest of tree-branches,
a swaying maze of gestures
eastways, westways.

Who knows which I am,
this criss-cross evening —
or how many?

THE SHADOW OF FIRE
(Ghazals)

Rockpool

My generation is dying, after long lives
swung from war to depression to war to fatness.

I watch the claws in the rockpool, the scuttle, the crouch —
green humps, the biggest barnacled, eaten by seaworms.

In comes the biggest wave, the irresistible
clean wash and backswirl. Where have the dead gone?

At night on the beach the galaxy looks like a grin.
Entropy has unbraided Berenice's hair.

We've brought on our own cancers, one with the world.
I hang on the rockpool's edge, its wild embroideries:

admire it, pore on it, this, the devouring and mating,
ridges of coloured tracery, occupants, all the living,

the stretching of toothed claws to food, the breeding
on the ocean's edge. 'Accept it? Gad, madam, you had better.'

Eyes

At the end of winter my self-sown vine sends up
sprays of purple flowers, each with two green eyes.

Driving home in the night I startled a fox.
The headlights fixed him staring and snarling back.

There's altogether too much I know nothing about:
my eyes slide over signals clear to the fox.

But what I do see I can fix meanings to.
There are connections, things leave tracks of causation.

The fox-trot marks in the hardened silt of the road
led to those chicken-feathers caught in the fence.

The fox's two green eyes echo his universe;
he can track rabbits better than I can foxes.

But I saw the chicken-feathers caught in the fence;
and fox, I know who's looking for you with a rifle.

You know no better than the two green eyes on the pea-flower
the link between the feathers and the sound of the shot.

Rockface

Of the age-long heave of a cliff-face, all's come down
except this split upstanding stone, like a gravestone.

Sun-orchids bloomed here, out and gone in a month.
For drought-stricken years, I haven't seen those flowers.

In the days of the hunters with spears, this rock had a name.
Rightly they knew the ancestral powers of stone.

Jung found in his corner-stone the spark Telesphorus.
Earth gives out fireflies, glow-worms, fungal lights.

Walking here in the dark my torch lights up
something massive, motionless, that confronts me.

I've no wish to chisel things into new shapes.
The remnant of a mountain has its own meaning.

Summer

This place's quality is not its former nature
but a struggle to heal itself after many wounds.

Upheaved ironstone, mudstone, quartz and clay
drank dark blood once, heard cries and the running of feet.

Now that the miners' huts are a tumble of chimney-stones
shafts near the river shelter a city of wombats.

Scabs of growth form slowly over the rocks.
Lichens, algae, wind-bent saplings grow.

I'll never know its inhabitants. Evening torchlight
catches the moonstone eyes of big wolf-spiders.

All day the jenny-lizard dug hard ground
watching for shadows of hawk or kookaburra.

At evening, her pearl-eggs hidden, she raked back earth
over the tunnel, wearing a wide grey smile.

In a burned-out summer, I try to see without words
as they do. But I live through a web of language.

Connections

The tiny clusters of whitebeard heath are in flower.
Their scent has drawn to them moths from how far away?

When I look up at the stars I don't try counting,
but I know that the lights I see can pass right through me.

What mind could weave such a complicated web?
Systems analysis might make angels giggle.

A child, I buried the key of a sardine tin.
Resurrected, I thought, it might unlock the universe.

Picking up shells on the beach, said Isaac Newton.
Catch a modern physicist using such a comparison.

I can smell the whitebeard heath when it's under my nose,
and that should be enough for someone who isn't a moth;

but who wants to be a mere onlooker? Every cell of me
has been pierced through by plunging intergalactic messages,

and the cream-coloured moths vibrate their woollen wings
wholly at home in the clusters of whitebeard heath.

Oppositions

Today I was caught alone in a summer storm
counting heartbeats from flash to crash of thunder.

From a small plane once I looked down a cliff of cloud.
Like God to Moses, it exploded into instructions.

Home, a yellow frog on the shower-pipe
startled my hand and watched me as I watch lightning.

Frog, my towel is wet, my hair dripping,
but you don't for such reasons take me to be a refuge.

Small damp peaceful sage with a loony grin,
('one minute of sitting, one inch of Buddha')*

a long time back we clambered up the shore
and learned to play with fire. Now there's no stopping us.

Back to the drainpipe, frog, don't follow me.
I'm off to dry my hair by the radiator.

I can't believe that wine's warm solaces
don't help the searcher: the poet on the wineshop floor

was given his revelations. The hermit of Cold Mountain
laughs as loudly perhaps — I choose fire, not snow.

* Manzan (1635–1714)

Memory

Yesterday wrapped me in wool; today drought's changeable
  weather
sends me down the path to swim in the river.

Three Decembers back, you camped here; your stone hearth
fills with twigs and strips peeled from the candlebark.

Where you left your tent, the foursquare patch is unhealed.
The roots of the kangaroo-grass have never sprouted again.

On the riverbank, dead cassinias crackle.
Wombat-holes are deserted in the dry beds of the creeks.

Even in mid-summer, the frogs aren't speaking.
Their swamps are dry. In the eggs a memory lasts.

They will talk again in a wet year, a year of mosquitoes.
The grass will seed on that naked patch of earth.

Now only two dragonflies dance on the narrowed water.
The river's noise in the stones is a sunken song.

Skins

This pair of skin gloves is sixty-six years old,
mended in places, worn thin across the knuckles.

Snakes get rid of their coverings all at once.
Even those empty cuticles trouble the passer-by.

Counting in seven-year rhythms I've lost nine skins
though their gradual flaking isn't so spectacular.

Holding a book or a pen I can't help seeing
how age crazes surfaces. Well, and interiors?

You ask me to read those poems I wrote in my thirties?
They dropped off several incarnations back.

Dust

In my sixty-eighth year drought stopped the song of the river,
sent ghosts of wheatfields blowing over the sky.

In the swimming-hole the water's dropped so low
I bruise my knees on rocks which are new acquaintances.

The daybreak moon is blurred in a gauze of dust.
Long ago my mother's face looked through a grey motor-veil.

Fallen leaves on the current scarcely move.
But the azure kingfisher flashes upriver still.

Poems written in age confuse the years.
We all live, said Bashō, in a phantom dwelling.

Pressures

Winter gales, spring gales, summer — under such pressures
the contours of things crouch, their angles alter.

The sapling that yesterday cut this view with a vertical
today is very slightly leaning eastward.

Brown butterflies strike my window-pane —
when I get up to look they have always become dead leaves.

Gravity's drag, time's wear, keep pressing downwards,
moving loose stones downslope, sinking hills like wet meringue.

I move more slowly this year, neck falling in folds,
pulses more visible; yet there's a thrust in the arteries.

Blood slows, thickens, silts — yet when I saw you
once again, what a joy set this pulse jumping.

Winter

Today's white fog won't lift above the tree-tops.
Yesterday's diamond frost has melted to ice-water.

Old age and winter are said to have much in common.
Let's pile more wood on the fire and drink red wine.

These hundreds of books on the shelves have all been read
but I can't force my mind to recall their wisdom.

Let's drink while we can. The sum of it all is Energy,
and that went into the wood, the wine, the poems.

Logs on the fire burn out into smoke and ash.
Let's talk today, though words die out on the air.

Out of the past and the books we must have learned something.
What do we know, what path does the red wine take?

I cleared white hair from my brush on the dressingtable
and dropped it into the fire. Some protein-chains the less.

How long would my hair be now if all the clippings
from the salon-floors returned to join their links?

The paths that energy takes on its way to exhaustion
are not to be forecast. These pathways, you and me,

followed unguessable routes. But all of us end
at the same point, like the wood on the fire,

the wine in the belly. Let's drink to that point — like Hafiz.

Patterns

'Brighter than a thousand suns' — that blinding glare
circled the world and settled in our bones.

Human eyes impose a human pattern,
decipher constellations against featureless dark.

All's fire, said Heraclitus; measures of it
kindle as others fade. All changes yet all's one.

We are born of ethereal fire and we return there.
Understand the Logos; reconcile opposing principles.

Perhaps the dark itself is the source of meaning,
the fires of the galaxy its visible destruction.

Round earth's circumference and atmosphere
bombs and warheads crouch waiting their time.

Strontium in the bones (the mass-number of 90)
is said to be 'a good conductor of electricity'.

Well, Greek, we have not found the road to virtue.
I shiver by the fire this winter day.

The play of opposites, their interpenetration —
there's the reality, the fission and the fusion.

Impossible to choose between absolutes, ultimates.
Pure light, pure lightlessness cannot be perceived.

'Twisted are the hearts of men — dark powers possess them.
Burn the distant evildoer, the unseen sinner.'

That prayer to Agni, fire-god, cannot be prayed.
We are all of us born of fire, possessed by darkness.

THE WEARING STRAND

Heloise Wakening

No, I would not go back there if I could.
The fire, as I recall it, sprang too high,
was something out of reason, passing God.
It fused us to a single blasphemy.

After, I thought: what snatched us to its height
and chars us in our separation now,
was some foreseeing of a fiercer light
than these insipid candles dare allow –

some future not yet possible, some Name
no saint or hermit knows or can conceive ...
An easier God's virago, I grow tame –
herding these simple nuns, who can believe

that flesh and spirit are not one, but two,
and one a slave to set the other free –
poor fools. We once had other work to do;
or so we thought. But who indeed were we?

It was as though all earth sent up a blaze
made of its very thought, to touch the sun,
and we that upward leap. No nights, no days
in that conjunction.
                    Heloise, have done.

The timid sister knocking at your door
wakes you, she thinks, to give yourself to God.
Go pray and scold again, His virgin whore,
and swear, you'd not go back there if you could.

For the Quaternary Age

When I looked down above the China Sea
on archipelagos of sullen pearl
and gaps of ocean flicked by sunlight's fin
it set me staring downwards into me.

Quaternary Age that made me in your dream,
fertile and violent, swung from ice to heat
to flood to famine – what you've grafted in!
Could I be calm when you are so extreme?

You tried to drown me in your melt of flood
and freeze me staring in your glacial step.
Burned by your intermitting fires I've known
splinters of crystal forming in my blood;

oppressed by shifts of rage and spells of calm
I felt your lightning spread my limited skull,
setting me tasks no wisdom would have done,
thrusting in probes, filling the wounds with balm.

You teach apocalypse and hymns of praise,
the use of fire, methods of stone and steel,
sacrifice, surgery, physics, the worship of sun.
Bound to your flying heels we wreck our days.

Your unpredictable dealings drive us wild.
We haruspicate, compute and pray your weather,
retreat to hive in cities, foul nests of men.
But here in this dragon-shell I'm still your child,

adoring this sudden light, the gaps between
terrors, the glow of cloud-tops, crevices
of green serenity. Whimpering, half in love,
I press on the armoured glass to watch you, lean
to your diverse passages, asking what you mean
by those mute and merciful designs of pearl.

You knock me back with a fang-flash and a snarl.

For M. R.

All summer the leaves grow dense, the water-lilies
push up arrowhead after arrowhead,
burst into smoke-blue, hit the central gold
and then retract themselves into bulb and mud.
Coming round the world, another season begins.

Martin, we have been writing to each other
for years, telling joys, griefs, happenings,
family gossip. Lives don't fit into letters
over one-half of the world. But talking over that space
we've been – what was it Plato said? –
happy companions in our pilgrimage.
You are English, Norman, Greek.
I battle that heritage
for room in another country, want to speak
some quite new dialect, never can;
it grows from my roots, it is my foliage.
Any time I flower, it's in the English language.

When all the living's done
it's poems that remain.
All that is personal, said Yeats,
soon rots
unless packed in ice and salt.
Poems can chill, shock,
stop you cold in your tracks,
functional as an axe.
But, too,
are a centring blaze in the field,
a sudden positive shape
sprung from the crowding leaves.

Reading your letters' news
I'd come on a poem. I felt
through the foliage of our lives
(and more than once is luck for any poet)
the arrow sprung to the target,
the shaft trembling in the central gold.

Falls Country

(For Peter Skryzneçki)

I had an aunt and an uncle
brought up on the Eastern Fall.
They spoke the tongue of the falls-country,
sidelong, reluctant as leaves.
Trees were their thoughts:
peppermint-gum, black-sally,
white tea-tree hung over creeks,
rustle of bracken.
They spoke evasively,
listened to evident silence,
ran out on people.

She hid in her paintings,
clothed, clouded in leaves;
and her piano
scattered glittering notes
of leaves in sunlight,
drummed with winter rains,
opened green depths like gullies.

He took better to horses;
the galloping storms of hoofs,
like eucalypts chattering,
or stones hopping on slopes.
Enclosed in the dust of mobs
or swinging and propping
among those ribbony boles
he was happy.
His eyes were as wary,
as soft as a kangaroo's.

Snow falling, the soft drizzle
of easterly weather
covers them, my old darlings.
What does the earth say?
Nothing sharp-edged.
Its gossip of lichen and leaf
its age-curved granites
its glitter of wetness
enclose them.

Is the spring coming?
Are there hooded orchids?
That's what their bones breed
under the talk of magpies.

Listen. Listen,
latecomer to this country,
sharer in what I know
eater of wild manna.
There is
there was
a country
that spoke in the language of leaves.

Half Dream

Half dreaming half awake
I felt the old boat rock at the lake shore,
small pulse of waves in the moon-road
slop, lip, withdraw,
pull and slack of the rope,
sigh in the trees.
Old boat
nibbles her rope, swings;
black swan stirs asleep.
Rise, fall of breath,
hesitant regular beat.
Tug on the wearing strand
all night long
sidling, slackening.

A peaceful dream. No sound
but leaf-talk, lip on sand,
shift of swan-wing.
Half-awake my heart
tested its moorings, turned
back to sleep.
Let the breath rise and fall,
the regular ripple and slack
fray at the strand.